ROCK AND ALPINE PLANTS

ROCK AND ALPINE PLANTS

Ethne Clarke

WITH A FOREWORD BY
MAX DAVIDSON

This edition first published in 1996 by the
Promotional Reprint Company Ltd,
Deacon House,
65 Old Church Street,
London SW3 5BS
exclusively for Chapters in Canada
and Chris Beckett Ltd in New Zealand.

ISBN 1 85648 296 0

Publishing Manager *Casey Horton*
Editor *Jennifer Spaeth*
Designer *Ming Cheung*

Publisher's Note
Readers should note that plant breeders introduce new cultivars all the time.
Please check your seed catalogues for the latest ones.

WARNING
If using chemical herbicides,
fungicides or insecticides, be sure to
follow exactly the manufacturer's
instructions

Printed and bound in Hong Kong

CONTENTS

FOREWORD

The name rock plants can be very deceiving, as some people have the completely wrong impression that you need a pile of large stones in order to grow these fascinating plants. Rock plants are simply any plant which is small in stature, making it suitable for growing in contained landscapes.

Alpines, on the other hand, are best thought of, in most cases, as the mountain relatives of many of the herbaceous perennials which we grow in the border of our gardens.

As such both are perfect for small beds and for growing in all sorts of containers. The great advantage, however, of alpines over most perennials is that most are evergreen and provide something of interest even in winter. Some also have an incredibly long flowering season, which stretches from spring until autumn. But there are also a huge number of them which provide flowers too in summer and autumn.

Most alpines, however, are at their best in spring, when they break out in a sudden rainbow of color.

Some alpines are true, mat-forming dwarfs, which hug the contours of the ground or creep over low walls. Others are large and surprisingly vigorous, so do check carefully on the anticipated size the plant is expected to reach when it is set out in your garden. Some species of a particular plant can be dainty while others can be relative giants. The problem is that alpines look so appealing in their small pots at the garden centre that it can be extremely difficult, without doing some prior homework, to avoid the invasive monsters, which need constant cutting back.

There are alpines which are happiest when planted in soil and surrounded by grit, and others which thrive in the glacial scree. Some relish shade, while others like to grow on rock surfaces in full sun.

Alpines originate from an environment with extreme climatic changes – from the hot-midday sun of a mountain top to cold alpine nights. However, once planted in a gritty, free-draining loam compost and surrounded by even more of that soil, which keeps the roots cool in summer and protects the plants from the brutal winter wet, most alpines will be happy.

I also recommend them on their price. You can fill a container with alpine or rock plants, which will last for years, for little more than the cost of buying some annuals for just one season.

Another advantage of alpine plants is that they need very little feeding apart from the occasional use of a general liquid fertiliser in spring, especially one of those which have a wide range of trace elements in addition to the usual nitrogen, phosphorus and potash. It is also their ability to go without regular watering which make the alpines such ideal candidates for modern gardens.

I would never be without my alpine or rock plants as they are among the prettiest plants to grow in the garden.

MAX DAVIDSON

INTRODUCTION

In his book *Garden Construction*, published in 1923, garden writer T. Geoffrey Henslow wrote: 'To own a lovely garden or beautiful estate and not possess a rock garden is more than being out of fashion; it is the loss of a joy that might easily be ours at small cost and little trouble. We are not called upon to climb the Alps for rare plants or to search the Andes for the latest novelties, since this has been done for us, and most of our English nurseries supply collections large enough to please the most exacting.'

More than seventy years later, things have changed somewhat on the garden scene and rock gardens are not the hot item in garden fashion they once were. However, alpine and rock plants still have a certain cachet, especially if you grow the cushion-forming sorts as specimen plants in sink gardens, and there are still plenty of nurseries to satisfy demand.

Today's gardeners want to grow a wide variety of plants in their gardens, which, in most cases, are usually an easy-to-manage parcel of land, hardly the place to install the traditional rock garden of tonnes of raw stone heaved into a semblance of an alpine rock face. Do not despair though, in this book you will see that it is possible, without too much work, to have a lovely rock garden.

Rock constructions have featured in gardens for centuries, but the rock garden, or rockery, really came into its own in the mid-1800s. People undertaking the Grand Tour often included a walk in the Alps and, marvelling at the plants they encountered and the beauty of their setting, sought to recreate a corner of this environment. By the early 1900s, there were many garden design firms all advertising their ability to construct superior rock gardens.

Nowadays, a rock garden is bound to be a more modest affair assembled by the garden owner rather than a garden contractor. This is not necessarily a good thing, because it is all too easy to make a rock garden which looks more like a pile of rubble rather than a carefully constructed landscape feature.

You must be prepared to invest in proper rock, quarried for the purpose, as a rock garden cannot be made from chunks of broken-up concrete paving or heaps of clinker. One other aesthetic rule to bear in mind, for even the slightest bit of authenticity, is that a rock garden needs to be built into a slope, so that the imitation rock outcrops don't look like a mineral carbuncle on your private landscape. Since most of us have flat gardens this can be rather difficult, but can also be overcome. You can excavate to alter the levels of your ground or you can erect low, dry stone walls to make raised beds. The most successful alternative, in my opinion, is the scree bed, which is an emulation of the free-draining gravel and broken rock that accumulates at the foot of a rock-face. A flat carpet of stone, sprinkled with rock garden plants, upon which pots and pans of choice alpine can be stood, is also an exceedingly pretty sight.

In the United Kingdom, the most highly-prized rock for gardens is the limestone of Lancashire, Derbyshire and Cumbria, but a recent report highlighted that there are less than 2500 hectares of this limestone left, with less than three per cent of this amount remaining undamaged by dealers quarrying it to supply the demand of rock garden fanciers. All responsible gardeners, no matter where they garden, will appreciate how wrong it is to despoil an area of natural beauty for the sake of something as transient as a garden. If, however, you are determined to have a rockery, try to purchase materials that you know are quarried by license or are otherwise eco-sound.

ROCK GARDEN DO'S AND DON'TS

I CANNOT THINK OF ANOTHER AREA of garden-making with as many rules about what you can and cannot do to have a successful garden than rock and alpine plant gardening. They are serious rules which, if broken, ensure failure – you have been warned.

Just as you cannot use old building rubble to build the rock garden, you can and should use local stone because that is what will look natural. Even though what you are about to construct is an artificial element in the landscape, you must strive to make it look natural.

There are five main types of rock. Granite is the hardest and weathers slowly. Slate is the next hardest and is unusual for its gradations of colour from a dark grey-green to nearly black. Limestone is quite soft and weathers well, but you must take care not to grow lime-hating plants, while sandstone is probably the softest type of all. Tufa is a sort of limestone which lime-hating plants will tolerate; it looks like a sponge and does, in fact, hold masses of water.

The site of a rock garden is important. It must not be in the shade or under the drip of overhanging trees. Preferably, it should be in full sun, although part shade is acceptable. A shelter belt of evergreen shrubs or trees on the side of the prevailing wind will give protection from damaging winter winds.

Perfect drainage is absolutely critical, because if there is one thing alpine plants will not tolerate it is sodden soil. Paradoxically, they do like to have plenty of moisture during the growing season, but the water must not linger. To avoid this, you must provide a free-draining soil with plenty of humus in the compost mix.

Regarding compost, most alpines like lime, so will do well in alkaline soils, while a few must have an acid soil. Generally, lime-loving plants will grow in soil that is slightly acid. Soil alkalinity is expressed in degrees of pH, from 0-14, a pH of 7 being neutral. Above that number the soil is

ABOVE: Use stone troughs to house lime-hating alpines, or bed them onto slabs of tufa to provide the free-draining conditions they require.

RIGHT: Alpine troughs make stunning features in sloping rock and alpine gardens.

progressively alkaline, below it is acid. The pH can be tested by means of easy-to-use testing kits available from garden centres, so prepare your compost according to the plants you intend to grow.

Composts can be purchased specifically for growing alpine plants and for growing lime-hating alpine plants (this will be identified as ericaceous compost), but you may want to blend your own, especially if you require a considerable quantity. The basic ingredient of compost is loam or clean topsoil, free of weed seeds and soil-borne pests; then moss peat (not sedge peat which is very acidic) or well-rotted garden compost; then grit or sand. Never use yellow builder's sand for horticultural purposes. The proportions are 2:1:1. When blending the compost add a few generous handfuls of bone meal.

Most alpines you purchase will be container-grown, which means that you can plant them at any time of year. However, it is always best to plant either in the autumn or spring, when nature will help you with the watering and when there is less risk of dry hot spells. If you do plant during the height of summer, water the plants daily and give temporary shade for the first few days in their new home.

Most garden centres provide a selection of rock garden stone, but it may be less expensive to go direct to a local supplier or quarry. That way, too, you can be assured of obtaining local stone. The cost of haulage can be quite steep, so the closer to home you obtain your stone, the less expensive it is likely to be.

Always use the same type of stone throughout a rock garden and be sure to obtain a range of sizes. You will need a team of at least three people – using trolleys, wheelbarrows and crowbars – to shift the largest rocks. To a large extent, a successful finish will depend upon how carefully you place the rocks, with an eye to keeping their natural strata aligned and, just as important, their relation to one another in proportion. To do this you will need two people to coax the rocks into the desired placings, while you stand back and, with your expert's eye, direct operations. Seriously though, in this case, many hands really do make light work and you will need to step back frequently to assess the positioning of the rocks.

All too often I see rock gardens, which look horribly unnatural because each stone is placed in lonely isolation, plopped down and separated from its neighbours by a foot or more of soil in which a miserable little plant appears aimlessly adrift. Fortunately, there is more artistry to creating a rock garden than that. To get a clear idea of what I mean, make a visit to your local botanic garden and study how they have positioned the rocks in carefully arranged outcrops, partially buried in the surrounding soil so

ABOVE: If creating a rock or alpine garden from scratch is not your choice, you can still grow a wide range of alpines in shallow terracotta pots and pans.

RIGHT: A scree garden made from a mix of rocks and gravel is an attractive garden feature.

that the rocks appear as they would in nature. Also notice how the lines and fissures – the strata – of the rocks all run in the same direction and how each rock is tilted back ever so slightly to assist water run-off. These botanic garden creations will no doubt be much larger than anything you will be attempting, but the rules of construction are the same for five stones as for fifty. Remember, you are trying to mimic nature, so you must either observe what nature does or study what professional rock garden makers have done.

Constructing a Rock Garden

Remember, drainage is critical, so unless you are building your rock garden into an existing steep slope, chances are you will have to improve the bottom drainage. To do this you must excavate the site of the new rock garden to a depth of about 25 cm/10 in and then backfill with a 10 cm/4 in layer of rubble, over which you spread a 5 cm/2 in layer of sharp sand. Top off with a 10 cm/4 in layer of clean topsoil.

The easiest way to make a rock garden on a flat site is in a series of tiered terraces. Place the stones carefully, making sure that markings and so on fall naturally; butt the stones up against each other and bury them into the prepared site by about one-third of their total size. Try to make the stones look as though they were being pushed up out of the soil. They should also tilt back slightly, rather than lay flat. Fill in and around the

RIGHT: Often it is possible to create the rock garden at the edge of a lawn where it slopes gently to meet the paving or terrace near the house.

BELOW: The stunning *Polygonum vaccinifolium* makes a blanket of poker flowers; unlike dainty true alpines, some rock plants are rampant and will have to be thinned out from time to time.

stones with prepared compost, firming the soil well into place. Repeat this process with the remaining tiers, partially burying each stone and firming the soil well to ensure there will be little or no movement. When you have completed the construction, water the rock garden well and leave for a few days before planting. This will allow the rocks and compost to settle and permit you to top up with compost before planting.

The only planting that you should do as you progress is that of crevices and cracks created where the stones butt up against each other. It is not,

ABOVE: Take care to position stones naturally and to plant generously so that the planting will quickly soften the appearance of the stones as these clumps of armeria and veronica are doing.

BELOW: **Stone walls can be turned into rock gardens and many plants are suited to this habitat, creating flowering curtains that will shroud the stones in bright colours.**

by any means, desirable to plant every one of these, but do use the opportunity to cultivate a few specimens, such as sedums and sempervivums.

As I mentioned before, the ideal rock garden is one built into a slight slope, but unless this slope is composed of free-draining, sandy soil you will still have to improve the drainage conditions by excavating as described above. Begin work at the top of the slope and work downwards to make the task easier.

ALTERNATIVE ROCK GARDENS

THE GREAT THING ABOUT ALPINE AND ROCK plants is that they are so collectable. Like doll house furnishings, 00-gauge model trains and other small toys, it is probably their miniature stature that makes these dainty plants so desirable. However, you may catch the rock plant bug, but not the rock garden fever, in which case you can relieve your symptoms by cultivating the plants in a number of alternative situations, which I discuss here.

Sink Gardens

After true rock gardens, sink gardens are the most popular artificial habitat for alpine and rock plant collections. Once again, I recommend a visit to your local botanic garden to see how the sink gardens there are composed. You will see wonderful miniature landscapes complete with dwarf trees, shrubs, herbaceous plants and bulbs. It is quite spellbinding and reminds me of the miniaturised landscapes of the Japanese bonsai gardens, but that is another kind of gardening altogether. Nevertheless, the aesthetic values remain the same – landscaping materials, plants and the scale of all the parts must be in harmony.

ABOVE: **Old-fashioned stone sinks are highly desirable for making alpine gardens.**

RIGHT: **Stone sinks fit nicely into the garden scenery mixing naturally with the other rocks.**

Once upon a time it was possible for gardeners to obtain true stone sinks, but the increasing popularity of this style of garden meant that demand soon outstripped supply. It is still possible to obtain stone sinks, but at an exorbitant price, and generally from antiques dealers – just to give you an idea of how far up the ladder of desirability stone sinks have climbed in recent years.

ABOVE: The tiny scale of a sink garden should be respected, and only small plants grown.

LEFT: A collection of stone sinks makes a nice focal point.

Hard on the heels of the true article came the white enamelled sinks, stripped from old kitchens in the name of modernisation (it is amusing that contemporary versions of these sinks are now offered by fitted kitchen designers). These sinks, however, can be covered in a hypertufa mix to make a passable imitation stone sink.

19

MAKING A HYPERTUFA SINK

You will need one plastic bucket, a sack of ready-mix cement, sedge or moss peat, builder's sand and a tub of general-purpose contact adhesive, such as Unibond.

Clean the sink, taking care to remove any trace of grease, dirt or scum and stand it on bricks to raise it off the ground.

Paint a layer of adhesive all over the exterior and over the top edge into the interior by about 10 cm/4 in. Apply it evenly but thickly and then scumble the surface with a garden hand fork.

While the glue begins to set, thoroughly mix together one part cement with one and a half parts peat and two parts sand. Then add just enough water to make a stiff, doughy paste. This is the hypertufa.

Test the surface of the glue. When it feels tacky, put on a pair of rubber gloves, take a handful of hypertufa and apply it to the sink. Apply an initial layer about 1 cm/½ in thick. It should be quite rough. Work from the bottom up, taking the mix over the edge to the interior of the sink, so that when it is filled with soil there will not be any white enamel showing to give the game away. Remember to keep the drainage hole free.

Let the sink dry for a few days, then move it into position. To help it acquire the patina of age, paint it over with plain yoghurt as described above. Alternatively, you can purchase a liquid ageing compound specially blended for the job.

If you don't have an enamel sink, you can still make a hypertufa version by using a box, of the correct size, as the mould. It is a method learned from a friend who is a sculptress; she advises using polystyrene boxes of the sort used to pack fish for market. However, you can use any size box – even ice cream cartons to make mini-sinks.

First you must wrap the box in small mesh chicken wire, moulding it closely to the sides, inside and out. This forms an armature upon which the hypertufa is shaped. Turn the box upside down and poke a large drainage hole through the bottom of the box. You can make several holes and keep them open by plugging them with short lengths of bamboo, which can be removed after the hypertufa is dry. Mix the hypertufa as before, but make it somewhat stiffer by using less water. Apply the hypertufa to the outside of the box first, patting it on evenly in small handfuls; try to keep it a uniform thickness so that it will dry evenly. Leave to set firm before inverting the 'sink' to complete the inside coating. When the inside coating is completed, leave

ABOVE: The material used to make artificial stone sinks is hypertufa. It can be moulded onto old ceramic sinks or cast free-form. It also allows the gardener another dimension of artistic creativity.

ABOVE: Here a hypertufa free-form basin houses a collection of succulent plants.

to dry thoroughly before removing the bamboo plugs, if used, and then paint with yoghurt to encourage lichen and so on.

Drainage in a sink garden is easier to control since the whole environment is artificial. First of all, though, remember the rule about positioning and site the sink in a sunny, open place. Do not set the sink directly on the ground, but instead prop it up on bricks. The sink should slope very slightly in the direction of the drainage hole to encourage water run-off. Cover the hole with broken crocks and put a layer of gravel in the bottom of the sink. Fill with compost (an extra handful or two of sharp grit added to the compost will further aid drainage).

Position the selected rocks, partially burying them just as you would for a full-scale rock garden. Keep it simple, however, and don't use so many rocks that it looks like a heap of rubble in a box. One or two perfectly formed specimens will suffice; choose them for their interesting shape or texture. Put in the plants and then cover the soil surface with a layer of washed gravel. Do not fill it to overflowing, but leave a gap of at least 2.5 cm/1 in between the surface of the soil and the rim of the sink.

Alpine plants need water at their roots and in a sink garden this can be difficult to achieve as water tends to run off the surface of a well-planted sink. This, however, can easily be overcome by building in a submerged irrigation outlet, this is a length of plastic drainpipe, about 5 cm/2 in in diameter, 'planted' in the corner opposite the drainage hole (it should be only as long as half the depth of the compost). Water into this tube and the roots will be well-irrigated. The top of the tube can easily be concealed by a small rock plug.

LEFT: If you are fortunate
enough to have a stone wall in
your garden, it makes a perfect
backdrop to herbaceous border
plantings and provides a home
for many sorts of rock and
alpine plants.

RIGHT: Stone walls often
provide moist, cool micro-
climates that suit plants such as
campanulas, periwinkles,
lamiums and lungworts. As
shown here, they make a very
naturalistic display.

BELOW: A low raised wall can
be used to edge a path and
create a sunken walkway
through the garden.

Dry Stone Walls and Raised Beds

Field boundaries marked by stone walls are a common landscape feature
in the country. A close inspection will reveal that these walls have been
colonised by plant communities, flourishing
in the perfect drainage and shelter the stone
fabric provides.

These walls can be translated to the garden
and used to create low terraces against
boundary walls or freestanding raised beds in
the garden. Raised beds are usually rectangu-
lar, although it is possible to build them in
curved shapes.

You can use real stone to make the walls,
or you can purchase reconstituted stone,
which is available in a variety of colours and
shapes. This is cheaper than real stone and
also easier to use since the blocks are more
uniform in shape and size.

If the wall is to be taller than 30 cm/12 in,
you must make a sound foundation by
digging a trench around the perimeter as
wide as the width of the wall and about 15
cm/6 in deep. Fill the trench with 5 cm/2 in
of rubble, which you must ram down well

into the bottom of the trench, and then cover this with concrete. When the concrete is set, lay the first course of stones and cement them to the foundation.

As you progress with each course, lay the stones so the wall slopes inwards slightly. Do not make the walls of a raised bed any taller than 1 m/3 ft tall; a run of dry stone wall for a terrace or retaining wall can be up to 1.2 m/4 ft tall. The finished width of a raised bed should be only about 1.5-1.8 m/5-6 ft, so that the centre can be easily reached from any side.

Part of the attraction of a stone wall is the planting, which can be done between the stones, so that you can have cascades of aubrietia, sprays of sedum and so on. It is very important to remember that any planting must be done while the wall is being made. Once the stones are in place it will not be possible to successfully introduce a plant's roots between the stones. So plant as you go, firming soil around the roots and between the stones.

When the raised bed is complete, fill it one-third full with clean rubble over which you then spread a layer of free-draining compost. Leave this to settle before planting, after which you finish off by spreading a 2.5 cm/1 in thick mulch of clean gravel.

The finishing touch is to make an apron of gravel around the base of the bed or along the wall footing. This will prevent the raised stonework looking like it was dropped by accident onto the lawn. The

ABOVE: Raised-bed rock garden planted with spring-flowering primulas, saxifragas and phlox.

RIGHT: Aubrietia flowers profusely in the spring and is a good companion for bulbs.

ABOVE: An extensive rock garden such as this is a source of inspiration even if your own patch is postage-stamp size.

gravel border also makes it easier to trim the lawn edge, prevents grass growing into the stones and generally makes for a neater appearance.

The apron should be 25-30 cm/10-12 in wide and the gravel layer about 7.5 cm/3 in deep. If you lay a ribbon of horticultural fabric mulch under the gravel it will help to suppress weed growth.

Scree Gardens

After all this talk about rocks we come to something rather more manageable – gravel, as used in making a scree garden. Scree refers to the mass accumulation of broken rock and small stones that naturally occurs at the foot of a rock or cliff face. It is the result of the natural degradation of the rock by weathering. The uppermost strata is dry and sunbaked, but the substrata is cool and moist because of the water run-off flowing from the mountainside and into the scree.

In the garden you can easily combine a scree with a rock garden in an imitation of nature, with one end of the rock garden seemingly disintegrating into a gravel carpet. But if you have no room or inclination for a rock garden, you can simply have a scree, perhaps as an apron around the house foundations, in which to grow alpine treasures or simple rock plants.

As with all forms of rock gardens, perfect drainage is vital, as is an open site away from overhanging trees. Mark out the shape of the scree garden just as you would any garden bed, except bear in mind that you are mimicking nature and in the mountains a scree fans outwards from the foot of the rocks. If you are making a scree garden in isolation, try to achieve a shape that looks like a spreading puddle of gravel.

To make a scree garden you must first remove the topsoil to a depth of 45 cm/18 in. This may take you into the subsoil, in which case prick it over with a garden fork, but do not dig it over. Backfill with 15 cm/6 in of clean rubble and compact this firmly into the bottom of the garden site. Finally, cover the rubble with a 5 cm/2 in layer of gravel and coarse sand.

To emulate the action of water running below the plants, you can install a drip hose irrigation system. During a drought this will help to ensure the plants remain watered at their roots, as overhead watering can be detrimental to many rock plants.

A drip hose system is easy to use. First, lay the hose over the gravel and sand, spacing it out according to the manufacturer's recommendations. Then cover the area with 2.5 cm/1 in layer of compost made from fine gravel, clean loam and peat in a ratio of 3:1:1. The hose should also be covered.

Finally, spread an even gravel mulch, up to 2.5 cm/1 in thick over the entire area. You can dot the scree with some interestingly shaped large boulders or with chunks of tufa rock, which have been planted up – there are many rock and alpine plants to choose from.

ABOVE: *Linum flavum*, with its canary yellow, glossy flowers is a simple rock garden plant that enjoys a scree garden.

RIGHT: A large scree garden such as this must have access paths running through; stone pavers are ideal for this.

LEFT: Raised peat gardens are essential if you wish to grow acid-loving plants but have alkaline garden soil. Wooden railway sleepers are much used to make the retaining walls for such gardens as the aged wood blends well with the peat.

Peat Beds

Rock gardening is a specialised pursuit. Gardening on a peat bed is even more specialised, for it provides acid soil conditions suitable for only certain plants. Traditionally, peat beds were formed using large chunks of peat rather than rocks to build terraces and outcrops. Today, however, it is rather difficult, and not really ecologically friendly, to obtain sizeable pieces of peat, so gardeners have turned to wooden alternatives. Railway sleepers are highly prized for making the retaining walls of a peat bed, but logs, stripped of bark and treated with suitable preservatives, are also widely used.

The rules for making a peat bed are different from the standard rock garden practice. First off, you should site the bed in a shady place since many peat-loving plants are woodland natives. They also like a moist soil, so drainage does not have to be perfect. Finally, and most critically, peat-loving plants cannot abide a chalky soil, so even though you will be establishing an island of acidity, if the soil in your garden is naturally chalky, with high alkalinity, I'm afraid your peat bed will be doomed to failure. As you water the garden, the moisture will pass through the peat bed and into the foundation, only to be reabsorbed by the peat. The water will have become alkaline and, in time, the build-up will adversely affect the growing conditions. If your soil is neutral or only slightly alkaline, there should be no problem. Also, it is much better to water with rain water, rather than tap water.

To construct a peat bed, clear the site of any perennial weeds and fork it over. Lay the peat blocks just as you would stones for a rock garden. If you are using sleepers or wooden logs, you will need to attach them to

ABOVE: Wooden planks and post uprights to support them make a natural retaining wall for a peat garden.

upright supports. Fill the bed with a compost mix of moss peat, humus or well-rotted compost and acid-free grit in a ratio of 2:1:1. After planting, cover the bed with a wood-bark mulch.

Alpine Houses and Frames

As you will discover when reading the next chapter, there are rock plants and alpine plants. In the later category, there are a number of choice plants known as high alpines that only the most dedicated of alpine gardeners will want to grow. If you intend to get serious about cultivating alpine plants, you will eventually want an alpine house.

This is like a greenhouse, but with various design differences. First, the ventilation is arranged differently, so that as well as roof vents there are vents along the sides of the house at the same level as the top of the staging. The pitch of the roof is quite low so that the plants in their pots are nearer to the light than they would be in a standard greenhouse with a conventionally pitched roof. To maximise the plants' exposure to sunlight, the alpine house should be aligned on a north-south axis with an entrance on the south side. With the exception of the roof pitch, a standard greenhouse can be modified to make a passable alpine house.

Staging is important and it is best to use metal staging with plunge trays full of clean sand. The pots can have their bases submerged, which helps to keep the soil cool and moist.

Alpine houses are unheated as their main purpose is to keep the plants

BELOW: **Alpine houses are for the most passionate alpine gardeners. The construction of the building is dedicated to providing the most demanding alpines with the maximum sunlight, freely circulating air and surface dryness that they require to do well.**

ABOVE: Alpine houses do not have to be obtrusive. This small alpine house blends in well with the scenery.

LEFT: In the alpine house, individual plants are given separate pots, which are plunged into sand or gravel to facilitate free drainage. Each is carefully labelled and the low windows opening along the back of the benches ensure free circulation of fresh air around the plants.

dry during autumn and winter when cold, wet conditions prevail. But that is not to say that they should not be frost-free. A thermostatic heating device, which will switch on when temperatures approach freezing, is therefore a worthwhile investment. In their native habitats, high alpines spend the winter under a blanket of snow, which serves as insulation from severe and damaging frosts. In the artificial atmosphere of a greenhouse, the temperatures can vary from daytime warmth to night-time freezing and it is just this sort of fluctuation that alpines cannot withstand.

A frame is a structure built at ground level, usually adjacent to a greenhouse or alpine house, along the north-facing side, made with wooden sides and a glass top. The floor of the frame is made of horticultural fabric mulch, over which is spread a thick layer of clean sand. A frame is used to protect pot- or pan-grown alpines, to raise cuttings or as a holding bay for newly acquired specimens awaiting good planting conditions. On dry, sunny days throughout the year, and when there is no threat of frost during winter months, the cover of the frame can be lifted to allow ventilation. This is also the practice with an alpine house. For alpine plants under glass the rule is: windows open unless it is freezing.

The other area where you might risk killing by kindness is watering. In the garden drainage must be perfect; similarly, pot-grown plants under glass must never become waterlogged. Therefore, the rule is to err on the side of safety and don't water unless you are convinced it is necessary.

Pot-grown alpines will, in time, outgrow their pots and pans and have to be upgraded to the next size container. It is best to do this in the early spring or when the plant has finished flowering.

Choosing and Maintaining Rock and Alpine Plants

BY THIS TIME YOU ARE PROBABLY wondering what exactly the difference is between an alpine plant and a rock plant.

Alpine plants are defined by their natural habitat; they are found growing in mountainous regions of the world, above the tree line but below the area where snow lies permanently on the ground.

Rock plants refer to any plant which is by nature small or dwarf in stature, making it suitable for cultivation in the miniature landscape of a rock garden.

Spring is a good time to purchase and plant both rock and alpine plants. Look for healthy specimens and ones that fill the pot comfortably; they

RIGHT: Sloping rock garden in its natural setting.

BELOW: Slow-growing, clump-forming evergreens such as the succulent sempervivums and mossy saxifragas are ideally suited for growing in shallow pots and pans.

have neither outgrown the pots they are in nor appear to be marooned in a sea of compost. If roots are emerging from the base of the pot, the plant is potbound. If there is a small mat of moss and lichen on the surface of the compost, you will know the plant has been neglected. It is not necessarily a good thing to buy the plant which has the most flowers or the biggest leaves; look instead for a plant that has healthy foliage and evidence of new, healthy growth.

With all these 'buyer beware' warnings, my best advice is to buy plants for rock gardens from specialist nurseries. These nurseries will offer the widest range, will be able to advise you knowledgeably about the requirements

of the plants in their collection and will be only too pleased to help you select the best plants for your purposes.

Although there are a few annuals and biennials, we will mostly be interested in the enormous range of perennials (some short-lived), shrubs and bulbs that can be grown in a rock garden. It has been said the average life span of a perennial alpine is seven years, but that is just an average as some specimens can live to a ripe old age; others you will have to keep an eye on and propagate in order to keep them in your garden.

ABOVE: **Sempervivums can be quite stunning when in bloom, as this *S. tectorum* shows.**

ABOVE LEFT: *Veronica prostrata's* **foliage (left) makes a good contrast with *Chamaecyparis obtusa* 'Fernspray' (right).**

Propagation

Once you have the garden established and your expertise evolves, you may want to turn your attention to increasing stocks of your collection; either by renewing plantings that are fading with age, sharing with fellow rock gardeners or simply selling (so that you can invest in a few more plants). Propagation is one of the joys of any type of gardening and the techniques for alpine and rock plants are the conventional methods of seed sowing, cuttings and division.

SEED SOWING
Most alpines will increase from seed easily as long as it is sown while still fresh. In fact, some seeds will germinate even before the pod is ripe, so eager are they to increase. Many alpine seeds will require a period of vernalisation – exposure to freezing conditions – achieved by placing the seed in a refrigerator for a few days or a week.

It helps to take a look at the seed; if it is flat it will germinate more readily if you take the time to sow it on its side or edge. Some seeds have long tails; if you poke the seed into the compost with this tail protruding,

ABOVE: **Sempervivum species in a terracotta pot.**

it will spiral as it dries and in the process twist the seed firmly and deeply into the compost.

Sow the seed in pots of sandy compost, cover with a mulch of fine grit and then put each pot into a frame or else cover with cling film. As soon as the seed germinates, remove the cover or else begin to ventilate the frame. As soon as the seedlings have developed two true leaves, they can be pricked out individually and put into larger pots to be grown on before planting out.

Do remember that only seed from species will come true and look just like the parent plant, although there may be some variation in the depth of flower colour or leaf markings. Seed from non-sterile hybrids will be mixed and you may surprisingly find your own treasure. Similarly, cultivars and forms will be like the parent but different in colour, form and markings. The only way to be sure of producing a plant that is identical to the parent is vegetatively, by cuttings or division.

CUTTINGS

There are two types of cuttings, soft tip and heel or semi-ripe. The former is taken from a healthy new shoot, preferably one which is not flower-bearing. Carefully strip away the leaves, leaving only a few healthy leaves at the tip. Then make a clean cut across the base of the stem directly below a leaf node (the place where the leaves are attached to the main stem). Dip

RIGHT: **Many carpeting plants will root as they creep along the ground and can be increased by severing the rooted plantlets from the parent and growing on in a new site. Others, like this saxifraga, will root quite easily from trimmings dibbled into moist potting compost.**

the cutting into hormone-rooting powder and insert the cutting into a loose, sandy cutting compost; a 1:4 peat/sand mix is good (but you will need to potup the cuttings quite soon after they have rooted into a more fertile potting mix). You must then cover the pots to retain moisture around the leaves, so that there is no chance of them wilting. Some gardeners use plastic bags, but I find the easiest way to cover pots is to use a 2 litre plastic drink bottle cut in half; they fit snugly into the top of a 7.5–10 cm/3–4 in flowerpot, turning them into miniature greenhouses. Stand the pots in dappled shade.

Semi-ripe (heel) cuttings are made from new season's growth that has had a chance to begin to mature, so that the base is becoming woody while the tip remains soft. These are taken by pulling the selected shoot

sharply down so that it comes away with a small tongue or heel of old wood. Trim the end of this small flap and, if necessary, remove the leaves as before. Dip the cut into hormone-rooting powder and potup and cover as before.

DIVISION

This is the easiest method of propagation, but is only possible with plants which make small plantlets around their base or whose crown gradually increases in size by developing new shoots around its edges. These can be separated into individual plants and grown on in pots or else planted where they are meant to grow. Some plants will also make new growths by sending out runners, which root wherever they touch the ground. Once these have made an adequate root system, they can be detached from the mother plant to grown on their own.

Some bulbs and corms can be increased by a kind of division; if you lift a mature bulb or corm, you may find that it has developed tiny bulblets or mini-corms around its base. Remove these carefully and grow them on in a nursery bed for two years or so until they are large enough to plant out.

A few plants produce suckers, which are rooted shoots that emanate from the plant's root system. These can be cut off and planted elsewhere.

ABOVE: Many alpines object to damp settling on their leaves, which can be a problem in an open situation like this sink garden. But the plants can be protected by covering the sink with a decorative cloche during wet spells.

BOTTOM RIGHT: White flies are usually found on the underside of leaves so take care to spray the entire plant.

Pests

Alpine and rock plants are no different from ordinary garden plants in the range of pests to which they are prone. A few samples of these pests are given below (in order by degree of horridness).

BIRDS

For some reason, birds find great sport in shredding cushion and mat-forming alpines and their favourite seasons for this seem to be spring and early autumn. Some people swear by black thread spun like a web across the rock garden; others use various bird-scaring devices. I have even seen one garden where each plant was given a protective helmet of chicken wire, which turned the garden into a weird sculpture park. Since there are only two seasons of main destruction, I suggest bird scaring tape, also known as humming tape. A few lengths of this stretched across the garden is no more obtrusive than any other device, yet is easier to install and remove. It also interferes less with your view of any ground-hugging plants you may have planted, since the tape must be at least 90-120 cm/3-4 ft above the ground. It does work.

SLUGS AND SNAILS

If you already garden, you will no doubt have developed your own line of defence against these creatures. Most people's chosen method usually involves a liberal scattering of slug pellets. Slug pellets are very effective but are also unsightly and can be dangerous to pets and small children if not used with care. Generally though, if the soil is sandy enough to provide perfect drainage and the grit around the plants sharp enough, this will deter slugs and snails to some extent since they do not like to slither across gritty places – it is very uncomfortable.

BELOW: **Green flies or aphids are sap-sucking insects that quickly weaken plants and spread disease.**

APHIDS OR GREENFLIES

These are common garden pests, against which there are a whole range of sprays and powders. Good garden hygiene helps to prevent infestations of these pests, so try to keep your rock garden clean of debris. Systemic sprays are especially effective, taken into the plant's system through the leaves, it kills the aphids as they suck the sap. In a alpine house you will have to fumigate, especially if many of the plants are hairy or tufted.

MICE

These are generally most troublesome with bulbs and corms. I once planted several handfuls of crocus species, some in the ground and some in pans and not one came up. The mice had taken the lot. Mousetraps can be used in both frames and alpine houses, but, unfortunately, I have yet to find a solution for the garden.

RED SPIDER MITES

These pests thrive in the dry, warm conditions of alpine houses, but if you keep your alpine house well-ventilated and spray to raise the humidity during summer, you should avoid infestations. Similarly, if the garden becomes overheated and dry hose it down, setting the spray to a fine mist.

A–Z of Rock and Alpine Plants

Acaena

Natives of New Zealand, acaenas are vigorous, ground-covering plants with long, trailing branches covered in small leaves and, in some species, bearing wonderful, tiny burr-like flowers. Look for *A. buchananii,* with its soft green foliage and brassy, little flowers. *A. microphylla,* which is the most commonly seen species, has stunning bronze-grey foliage and red, bristle-headed flowers. Also look for 'Copper Carpet', which is especially colourful. 'Blue Haze' is another good sort and is available at most garden centres.

ABOVE: *Acaena microphylla.*

RIGHT: *Arabis comcasica* **and aurinia.**

Acantholimon

Native to dry hills in the Near and Far East, it makes tussocks of spiky leaves. It can take as much heat and drought as you can give it. *A. glumaceum* makes dark green clumps of foliage topped by shocking, bright pink flowers.

Achillea

These are the miniature relatives of the common herbaceous border plant and, likes their big sisters, they enjoy full sun and meagre, dry soil. The flowers appear in spring and early summer, but because the foliage is so attractive they are useful members of the rock garden all year round. *A. ageratifolia* has finely cut foliage and large flowers. *A. clavennae* has oval leaves that are a particularly luminous silver-grey. *A. tomentosa* has fern-like, soft grey leaves that form a ground-hugging mat covered with bright yellow flowers.

Aethionema

This is a lime-loving plant, but it will tolerate neutral or slightly acid soils for a warm, sunny spot. *A. grandiflorum* makes small shrubs bearing sprays of bright pink flowers all summer. Plants of the Pulchellum Group within the species are smaller with flowers in shades of pale to rose-pink. 'Warley Rose' is a popular cultivar.

Alchemilla

Familiar to gardeners as *A. mollis*, the Lady's Mantle; the dwarf form, *A.alpina* is worth having in the rock garden for its dainty leaves; the reverse sides glisten like silver setting off the sprays of small, yellow-green flowers. *A. erythropoda* is another widely available species also suitable for the rock garden; its small leaves are bronze-green in colour.

Allium

There are a number of species of this bulb, which are all relatives of onions and garlic. *A. caeruleum* has bright blue flowers as does *A. cyaneum*, which is slightly lower-growing. *A. karataviense* has wonderful broad, grey leaves, tinged purple, and stubby flower stalks bearing pale, lavender-grey flowers.

ABOVE: *Aethionema grandiflorum.*

Alyssum (now known as Aurinia)

Mat-forming plants that are a mass of flowers in the spring. However, after the big show they are not particularly interesting, so don't put too much emphasis on Aurinia in your rock garden display. *A. saxatile* 'Compacta', 'Dudley Nevill' and 'Dudley Nevill Variegated' are all good, showy cultivars.

Anacyclus

A. pyrethrum var. *depressus* is a fully hardy, ground-covering plant for a sunny place in a scree garden or gritty soil. The flower buds are a deep crimson opening to white flowers.

ABOVE: **Spring-flowering**
Androsace pyrenaica.

Anchusa

One of the finest blue flowers in the rock garden, *A. caespitosa* makes a tuft of stiff, narrow leaves forming a rosette around the flower cluster. It needs deep soil for its long tap root.

Andromeda

A. polifolia 'Alba' and *A. p.* 'Compacta' are both good evergreen shrubs for the rock garden. Their glossy, dark green leaves provide a perfect setting for the clusters of tiny white or, in the case of 'Compacta', pink flowers that appear in the spring. It needs an acid, moist soil.

Androsace

All of the following plants are easy to grow, widely available and favourites in the rock garden for growing in gritty soil and in crevices. *A. carnea* makes a tuffet of narrow, dark green leaves around stems bearing tiny pink or white flowers. *A. cylindrica* grows best in crevices, where it will make a low rosette of grey-green leaves studded with clumps of pink or white flowers. *A. lanuginosa* makes trailing stems covered with silvery leaves and dainty, pink flowers. *A. pyrenaica* makes a pincushion of short, spiky green leaves, which in season are covered with single, white flowers. *A. sempervivoïdes* makes a rosette of smooth, flat leaves around short stems carrying small, pink flowers.

Andryala

Here is a small shrublet for a hot, dry position. *A. agardhii* has silver foliage and gold-tinted flowers.

Anemone

The small relatives of the Japanese windflower, *A. japonica*, are generally found on woodland edges and so appreciate cool, shaded positions in the rock garden. *A. apennina* grows from a tuberous rhizome and makes dainty, blue flowers. *A. ranunculoïdes* 'Pleniflora' has double, yellow flowers and it will work its way gradually through a rock garden on creeping, woody roots.

41

Arabis

Easy to grow and quite showy, the evergreen, mat-forming *A. caucasica* 'Rosabella' is covered in a mass of rich, pink flowers throughout spring and into early summer. 'Snowcap' is, as you would expect, a luxuriantly white-flowered cultivar. *A. ferdinandi-coburgii* 'Variegata' has insignificant flowers, but good green and white variegated foliage.

RIGHT: *Arabis aubrietioides* **'Rosabella' (pink) with** *Arabis caucasica* **(white) and** *Aubrieta deltoidea.*

Arenaria

In the genus there is plenty of variety and a plant for most situations. *A. balearica* makes a tissue of pale green foliage covered with tiny, white star-like flowers; let it cover a rock in cool shade. *A. purpurascens* makes a mat of evergreen foliage and is covered in early spring with masses of shiny, pink stellar flowers; grow it in full sun. *A. montana* particularly likes cool crevices and will reward you with a waterfall of bright white flowers in spring.

Armeria

A. juniperifolia (formerly known as *A. caespitosa*) makes an evergreen hummock of spiky leaves covered from late spring to early summer in bright pink flowers. *A. maritima* is best known as sea thrift, a seaside wild flower with pink flowers. 'Vindictive' has dark red flowers, or there is the white-flowered 'Alba'. The foliage is grass-like and the flower stalks are like drumsticks.

Artemisia

Best known as the sun-loving denizens of the herb garden, the species suitable for rock gardens retain their pungent scent and silvery foliage. *A. caucasica* (once known as *A. lanata*) is valued for its great spreading mounds of silver, feathery foliage. *A. schmidtiana* 'Nana' makes rosette mats of finely cut grey leaves.

ABOVE: *Gypsophila repens* **growing in front of** *Armeria* *maritima.*

RIGHT: *Aurinia saxatile.*

43

Aubretia

There are numerous named selections and clones of this common garden carpeting plant. Its sheets of flowers in shades of pink, mauve, purple, bright red and white are widely admired. It is only suitable for the largest rock garden or terrace, unless you keep its spread in check. Best in full sun and well-drained soil.

BELOW LEFT: Aubrieta.

BOTTOM: Aubrieta cascading over rockery.

BELOW: *Aubrieta deltoides* 'Red Carpet'.

ABOVE: Campanula growing in between sedum and anaphalis.

ABOVE: *Campanula pelviformis.*

Campanula

A cheerful introduction to summer, it grows easily in open, sunny places and most require only good drainage. **C. carpatica** makes a lovely hummock of tiny bells in various shades of blue, mauve, purple and white. **C. portenschlagiana**, in spite of its name, is the easiest to grow, making a mat of bright blue. **C. thyrsoïdes** is totally different since the yellow flowers are held aloft on stiff stems. There are many others, too numerous to describe here.

Cyclamen

These are my favourites for the rock garden (and the garden generally). They have excellent foliage, cheerful little flowers in white and many shades of pink and, best of all, spring-action seed pods. As the seed ripens, the flower stalk curls in tight against the corm and the moment the seed is perfectly ripe, it springs out, shooting the seed away from the mother, gradually colonising the area. **C. coum** flowers in winter and spring and the 'Pewter Group' are so-called for their heavily silvered foliage. The autumn-flowering **C. hederifolium** (formerly known as **C. neapolitanum**) is the one most commonly encountered and **C. purpurascens** flowers during the summer. They like well-drained, but moist soil with plenty of added humus, if necessary.

Daphne

These shrubs are much loved for the intense perfume they possess and for the charming, waxy flowers that appear from late winter to early spring. **D. blagayana** is ground-covering. **D. cneorum** makes a small evergreen bush. 'Eximia' makes trailing branches and **D. mezereum** is the one much used in old-fashioned cottage gardens. It is really rather tall for inclusion in the rock garden unless you keep it clipped back (by taking pieces for winter flower arrangements).

BELOW: *Dianthus deltoïdes* 'Vampire'.

Dianthus

D. x arvernensis, D. gratianopolitanus and the stunning **D.deltoïdes** are probably the best of the alpine pinks to begin with; all in shades of pink and white with mats of grey foliage and a clove-like perfume. They require sun and good drainage to do well.

Dryas

D. octopetala makes an evergreen mat of dark green, leathery leaves, which sets off the yellow-centred white flowers to perfection. These plants appear from late spring through early summer and it is an easy little plant to grow in sun and well-drained soil.

Erigeron

The small-growing sorts of fleabanes offer some good candidates for both rock and scree gardens. **E. aureus** has tiny, hairy leaves and bitty, yellow flowers. It dislikes any wetness, so is best on scree. **E. karvinskianus**, also know as daisy-gone-crazy, deserves its common name since it quickly seeds itself in cracks, crevices and gravel, covering itself in a dusting of small, pinky-white daisies.

ABOVE: *Dianthus deltoïdes* growing with *Spiraea japonica* 'Goldflame'.

RIGHT: *Gentiana acaulis.*

BELOW: *Gentiana acaulis* 'Krumrey'.

Erodium

There are plenty of species to choose from in this long-flowering genus, but do look out for **E. cheilanthifolilum** and **E. corsicum**. Both have nice flowers and foliage, but do best in pots or pans, so they can over-winter in the alpine house.

Gentiana

Most alpine gardeners pride themselves on their collections of gentiana, they are the *sine qua non* of

LEFT: *Gentiana sino-ornata.*

the rock garden, and are quite easy to grow as long as you pay attention to their pH requirements, which range from neutral to acid. They are best for a peat bed where they will also get the moisture they like. **G. sino-ornata** demands nothing less than perfectly drained, totally lime-free soil to produce the fabulous blue flowers for which it is prized. 'Inverleith' is the most spectacular. Less fussy is **G. acaulis**; the stemless, kingfisher-blue flowers rest on a mat of dark green leaves. The willow gentiana, **G. ascle-piadea**, makes long, whippy flower stems with blue or white flowers (**G.a. alba**). **G. x macaulayi** 'Kingfisher' is widely available and likes a good acid soil.

Geranium

Of all the hardy geraniums, **G. cinereum** is probably one of the daintiest, making a spreading rosette of thumbnail-size leaves crowned in summer by masses of cup-shaped flowers. It does well in full sun and in moisture-retentive soil. Look for the cultivar 'Ballerina', which has rosy-pink flowers with a wine-red web of veins spreading across the petals from the dark centre of each flower. The variety **G. c. subcaulescens** has similar characteristics but sports rich, magenta-tinted petals around an almost black central boss, which has a stunning effect.

Helianthemum

Commonly known as rock roses, these plants are good for scree and rock gardens or for growing in walls or dry banks. 'Ben Nevis' has dark green foliage and bright orange flowers. 'Jubilee' has yellow blossoms and the species **H. nummularium** and **H. oelandicum** ssp. **alpestre** are evergreen shrubs, dwarf enough for a sink garden.

BELOW: *Geranium cinereum* '**Ballerina**'.

Helichrysum

This is the genus that produces the dried flowers commonly known as Everlastings. For the rock garden, look for the species **H. bellidioïdes**, a carpet of grey-green leaves dusted over with papery white flowers. **H. milfordiae** makes a rosette of oval, woolly grey leaves and crimson buds that open to white flowers.

Hepatica

These plants like cool, moist soil that is rich in organic matter and also a position that offers partial shade. **H. nobilis** makes a mound of soft, green leaves covered in spring with many simple white flowers. There are also pink, lilac and blue forms as well as a choice of double-flowered sorts. The garden variety **H. n.** var. **japonica** is widely available and has dark, leathery, semi-evergreen leaves and lilac-blue flowers.

Hypericum

You often see St John's wort grown as hedging, but for the rock garden there are a few small-stature species available. **H. olympicum** makes a nice and tidy, little deciduous bush. It's upright stems are covered in tiny, short green leaves and bear lovely, single, large egg-yolk yellow flowers that bristle at the their centres with long, silky stamens. It will seed itself, but not invasively. Another species to try is the lovely **H. empetrifolium** 'Prostratum', which makes a low-spreading shrub with starry, yellow flowers. It can be tender so protect from frost.

ABOVE: *Hypericum olympicum* 'Citrinum'.

Leontopodium

If rock gardens had mascot plants, the edelweiss would unquestionably be it. **L. alpinum** is widely available and much loved for its clusters of woolly, silvery-grey flowers and clumps of grey-green foliage. It does best in open sunny places.

Leucanthemum (now known as Rhodanthemum)

L. hosmariense is a favourite rock garden plant, loved by many for the shimmering mat of silvery leaves and masses of bright daisy flowers it makes all summer. When it is happy, as it usually is when given plenty of sun and well-drained soil, it can become overbearing, but responds well to vigorous thinning.

Lewisia

L. tweedyi and **L. rediviva** are two of the most popular species for rock gardens, making basal rosettes of thick leaves and branched stems carrying pale pink to rich pink flowers. There are many named hybrids as well offering a good range of colour. Lewisias prefer a lime-free soil and do best in cracks and crevices where perfect drainage is assured for their deep tap roots.

Linaria

L. alpina, is an annual that will seed itself easily into nooks and crannies on the sunny side of the rock garden. It makes great whorls of grey, narrow leaves and racemes of tiny, snapdragon flowers in shades of purple and yellow.

Linum

L. flavum 'Compactum' is the species that makes what is probably the brightest yellow splash in midsummer. The flowers have a glossy radiance, which is complemented by the dark green foliage. It does well in any soil in the sun.

ABOVE: *Lysimachia nummularia* 'Aurea'.

Lysimachia

L. nummularia 'Aurea' is a freely-spreading, hardy perennial that will form mats of greenish-gold leaves, which are topped in summer by penny-sized yellow flowers – a real splash of sunshine in the rock garden. It likes a fair bit of moisture to do well and should be given a sunny spot as shade will encourage the leaves to go green. It can be invasive but can be kept in check by simply pulling up handfuls where it is not wanted.

Morisia

A real miniature, **M. monanthos** makes a prostrate creeping tuffet of green, studded with dainty, yellow flowers in late spring. However, this only happens if it has the exceedingly sharp drainage that it likes best, so plant in sandy soil.

Nierembergia

For a long flowering period, the mat-forming **N. repens** is hard to better. It is not altogether hardy, so plant in sheltered spots or give the underground, creeping roots some winter mulch protection and it will repay you with masses of brilliant white flowers.

Omphalodes

The gentian blue flowers on dark, wiry stems make **O. cappadocica** very desirable in the rock garden. It likes moisture and part shade to do well. **O. verna** has paler blue flowers and larger foliage.

Ononis

O. fruticosa is a deciduous shrub that looks like a bristle brush because of its finely divided, hairy leaves. It carries its bold clumps of lavender-pink flowers during summer and likes good drainage in a sunny position.

BELOW: *Oxalis adenophylla* on gravel mulching.

Origanum

O. dictamnus is commonly known as Cretan dittany and was a favourite windowsill plant in old cottages. 'Kent Beauty' makes a prostrate plant and is covered during summer in the characteristic fragrant, oval leaves of the oreganos. The flowers are quite showy with papery pink bracts like the flounces of a tulle ballgown. It is not hardy, so best grown in a pot to over-winter in the alpine house. **O. rotundifolium** is a hardy little shrub which has showy, green bracts disguising the pale pink flowers, which cover the shrub throughout the summer.

Oxalis

The species **O. adenophylla** makes clumps of grey-green clover leaves and lipstick-pink flowers in early spring; it also increases easily from the tiny bulblets that form around the base of the mother bulb. Another good species worth trying is **O. enneaphylla**, also known as scurvy grass. It makes wonderful silvery-grey leaves and pearly-pink flowers. Both species do best in full sun and need good drainage.

ABOVE: *Phlox douglasii* 'Crackerjack' on the edge of a raised bed.

BELOW: *Phlox douglasii* 'Boothman's Variety'.

Papaver

P. alpinum is a delicate little thing, short-lived but free-seeding. It makes a clump of grey leaves over which the papery, white flowers flutter on wiry stems. *P. miyabeanum* has a similar habit and lifespan, but their flowers are faded yellow.

Penstemon

These are perennial favourites in the flower border, but there are a few species that qualify for the rock garden. *P. hirsutus* 'Pygmaeus' is a hardy evergreen and makes a compact little plant; bearing characteristic tubular white flowers, tinted lilac-blue on the outer surface of the petals. *P. pinifolius* is larger growing and has pillar-box red flowers. *P. newberryi* f. *humilior* is a hardy, evergreen shrub that makes a mat of dark green painted over with rose-pink flowers in summer. All like good drainage and sun.

Phlox

P. caespitosa is a hardy evergreen that makes a neat mound of spiky, green leaves covered with mauve or white flowers during summer; it is good for the rock garden or alpine sink garden. *P. nivalis* 'Camla' is a popular evergreen that makes mounds of wiry stems carrying masses of cherry-pink flowers in early summer; this one likes rich, moist soil to do well. *P. douglasii*

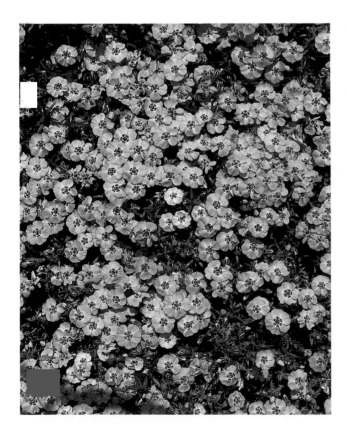

'Crackerjack' is also evergreen and the leaves all but disappear beneath the blanket of magenta-pink flowers in early summer. Clip over phlox after flowering to keep a neat shape.

Polygonum

P. vaccinifolium has a curious beauty with wiry, red stems holding aloft bright pink flower spikes above a neat carpet of evergreen foliage. The show begins in late summer at a time when the rock garden can be a little dull, so it is valuable for that reason as well.

Potentilla

The species suitable for the rock garden are mostly mat-forming perennials and flowers carried on long, arching stems. **P. alba** has white flowers. **P. aurea** has yellow. The hybrid, **P. tonguei**, has peach-coloured flowers and **P. megalantha** makes a mat of silver foliage with pink flowers nestling among the leaves.

ABOVE: *Pulsatilla vulgaris* **'Baron's Pink'.**

Primula

The great herald of spring in the garden, primulas have something to offer the alpine house with the graceful **P. allionii** and its numerous cultivars. It makes a mound of grey foliage smothered in flowers. Give it excellent drainage in a crevice and rich gritty soil and it won't let you down. **P. auricula**, **P. hirsuta**, **P. marginata** and **P. minima** are just a few of the many species that can be grown in the rock garden or alpine house.

ABOVE: *Pulsatilla vulgaris*

RIGHT: *Pulsatilla vulgaris rubra.*

BELOW: *Pulsatilla vulgaris* is a perennial plant.

Pulsatilla

The pasque flower, **P. vulgaris**, is widely available and there are quite a few cultivars to choose from when making a rock garden. Give them a good alkaline soil and full sun, and they will perform well.

Ranunculus

Some of the most interesting alpine and rock plants are found in this buttercup clan. **R. alpestris** is the alpine buttercup and the bright white, cup-shaped flowers are held above the glossy, dark green leaves for a long season; from late spring to midsummer. **R. ficaria albus** is a mat-forming perennial with similar glossy leaves and glossy, white flowers. Both these like moist soil and partial shade. **R. calandrinioïdes** is happier in sharply drained soil and sun; it has long, grey-green leaves and saucer-shaped, white flowers on long stems. **R. montanus** 'Molten Gold' has rich yellow flowers and dark green leaves all with the characteristic buttercup gloss.

Raoulia

While most alpine and rock plants are grown for their flowers, this genus is valued for the curiously tinted foliage of species like **R. australis, R. a.** Lutescens Group, **R. hookeri**, which come in varying shades of silvery-grey, and **R. haastii**, which makes a carpet of green in spring and gradually darkens to dark brown by winter. Please note that they need good drainage to keep their feet out of winter wet and gritty soil in sun or part shade.

Rhodohypoxis

A bulbous perennial that likes a sandy, acid soil and a sunny spot, but plenty of moisture during summer to do well. Not 100 per cent hardy, so plant in a sheltered spot. **R. baurii** is the most popular species, although **R. deflexa** offers a wide choice of cultivars, like 'Douglas' with cardinal red flowers.

Salix

There are some real curiosities among the willows, and a few of them are suitable shrubs for rock gardens. I fell for the weirdness of 'Boydii' with its gnarled, stubby stems and little, round, felted, grey leaves, but still have to find a place for it where the upright habit won't be too startling. **S. apoda** is prostrate and in spring male plants carry chubby catkins, like fat woolly caterpillars. **S. herbacea** barely lifts itself off the ground and is studded with acid-green catkins in spring. **S. lindleyana** also hugs the ground and has pink-tinted catkins. One of the prettiest of the prostrate willow tribe is **S. reticulata**, whose springtime flush of catkins is followed by the attractive, deeply veined, oval leaves cloaking the ground-hugging branches. They need moist soil and a place in the sun or part shade

Sanguinaria

Commonly known as bloodroot, this perennial creeps along by its rhizomatous roots, making clumps of grey-green leaves that complement the show of glistening, white flowers that often have a curious violet-blue or pink tinge on their reverse. It is hardy but needs moist, humus-rich soil and shade.

Saxifraga

This is one genus with plenty to offer the alpine and rock gardener; in fact you could be spoiled for choice. Because the genus is so diverse it is divided into several sections. The mossy saxifragas are the

ABOVE: **Alpines in a terracotta container – dianthus, sempervivum, raoulia and saxifraga.**

RIGHT: *Saxifraga granulata* 'Plena'.

ABOVE: *Saxifraga Granulata*, **known as meadow saxifraga.**

easiest group in cultivation, so these plants are a good introduction. Basically, they like a moist soil and a position where they will not be exposed to the baking sun. Gritty, alkaline soil also suits them well enough. A few good cultivars to look for are: 'Cloth of Gold', 'Bob Hawkins', 'Primulaize', 'Plena', 'Crenata', 'Cranbourne' and 'Gregor Mendel'. If you get hooked, a specialist nursery will help to sort you out.

Sedum

As for saxifragas, so for sedums. There are dozens to choose from and each as charming as the last. They like sun, but otherwise will tolerate even the most depressing soil conditions. Give them some care and they will reward you with an exhilarating variety of foliage and form; from the tiny, silvery-grey pebbles of **S. spathulifolium** to the long, flat tapering leaves, variegated pink and cream, of **S. kamtschaticum** 'Variegatum'. Again, turn to a specialist nursery for advice on which to choose.

ABOVE: *Sempervivum tectorum.*

ABOVE LEFT: *Sedum spathulifolium* 'Cape Blanco' on a wall.

BOTTOM LEFT: *Sedum spathulifolium* ssp *pruinosum* growing in gravel.

Sempervivum

Once again, a plethora of riches. Sempervivums are diverse and beautiful, love to be sunbaked and will tolerate the poorest soils. *S. tectorum*, the common houseleek, is a clump-forming rosette of succulent leaves that colonises the thatch and pantiles of old cottages. Look out for the lovely *S. arachnoideum*, called the cobweb houseleek, for the film of fine, white filaments knitted across the leaves. *S. montanum* makes rosettes, soft blue-green in colour and *S. giuseppi* has small, hairy rosettes that knit together to form a tight mat. Take advice from the specialists when choosing.

Sisyrinchium

Another large genus, but not overwhelming like the previous three. Sisyrinchiums have iris-like leaves, which shelter the demure flowers that are coloured shades of blue and violet; although there is a very desirable straw-coloured cultivar called 'Quaint and Queer'. *S. i dahoense* 'Album' has starry, white flowers for most of the summer and *S. macounii* has charming violet-blue flowers. They all need well-drained soil and a place in the sun.

Thymus

A favourite denizen of the herb garden and often recommended to edge paths and grow between paving stones. Some of the creeping thymes deserve to be in the rock garden, but there are so many to choose from. My favourite carpeter of all is the woolly thyme, **T. pseudolanuginosus**, and the variegated 'Doone Valley' makes a wonderful, neat mound of gold-variegated leaves. A good herb specialist will offer the widest choice. Full sun and dry conditions are needed.

LEFT: **Creeping thyme,** *Thymus serpyllum.*

BELOW: *Thymus serpyllum* **'Russetings'.**

RIGHT: *Veronica prostrata.*

RIGHT: *Veronica prostrata.*

Veronica

V. prostrata offers a wide range of cultivars in varying shades of white, blue, violet and pink. *V. pectinata* has trailing stems of violet-blue flowers and *V. filiformis* is one to watch out for because it is annoyingly invasive. Veronicas are very easy to please in any soil and sun.

ABOVE: *Viola riviniana* **Purpurea Group.**

RIGHT: *Viola tricolor* – **the common heartsease.**

Viola

V. riviniana Purpurea Group was previously known as *V. labradorica purpurea*. It is a little, clump-forming, hardy violet, which has dusky-purple foliage and deep purple flowers in early spring. It prefers retentive soil in the sun or part shade and when happy will seed itself around with gay abandon, just like its relative, *V. tricolor*, the common heartsease or Johnny Jump-Up. It is a familiar cottage garden flower, better known for its place in the herb garden rather than the rock garden.

ABOVE: *Zauschneria californica.*

Zauschneria

With a dry position in the sun, this curious plant will reward you with cascades of tubular, scarlet-red flowers. It is not entirely hardy so make sure there is some shelter for the plant. **Z. californica** 'Dublin' is one of the more flamboyant species.

INDEX

Picture Acknowledgments

The work of the following photographers has been used:
David Askham: 35, 44(tr); **John Baker**: 56(t); **Lynne Brotchie**: 16; **Linda Burgess**: 45(b), 51; **Chris Burrows**: 52; **Brian Carter**: 34(tr), 42, 46(b), 53(b), 54(t), 57, 60(t); **Bob Challinor**: 19, 55(b); **Jack Elliot**: 50; **David England**: 12, 24(t), 34(tl), 38, 39, 55(tl), 61(t); **Robert Estall**: 37(t); **Ron Evans**: 8, 27; **Christopher Fairweather**: 49; **John Glover**: 7, 10, 29, 30, 31, 33, 40, 41, 48, 58, 61(c); **Sunniva Harte**: 43(t), 46(c); **Neil Holmes**: 55(tr), 60(b); **Roger Hyam**: 59; **Lamontagne**: ii, 15, 22, jacket; **Jane Legate**: 36; **John Neubauer**: 20, 21; **Clive Nichols**: 24(b), 32; **Jerry Pavia**: 11; **Howard Rice**: 26, 53(t); **David H. Russell**: 54(b); **JS Sira**: i, 14, 37(b), 43(b), 47, 61(b); **Ron Sutherland**: 17, 22(b), 28; **Brigitte Thomas**: 6, 13, 18, 25; **Jonathan Weaver**: 56(b); **Micky White**: 44(tl); **Didier Willery**: 45(t), 46(t); **Steven Wooster**: 9, 23, 34(b), 44(b).

The following gardens were photographed:
Botanical Garden, Bronx, NY, USA: ii; **Cefn Bere, Wales**: 9; **High Meadow, Surrey, England**: 10; **Chelsea Flower Show 1989, London, England**: 17; **Woodpeckers**: 27; **Ambleside Road**: 31; **RHS Wisley**: 29; **Turn End Garden, England**: 32; **Bryn-y-Bont, Gwynedd, Wales**: 33; **Mien Ruys Garden**: 34(b); **The Fens Nursery**: 43(t), 46(c).